Seven Pals

by Greg Frazier
illustrated by Jennifer Emery

Core Decodable 60

Mc Graw Hill Education

Bothell, WA • Chicago, IL • Columbus, OH • New York, NY

MHEonline.com

Send all inquiries to:
McGraw-Hill Education
8787 Orion Place
Columbus, OH 43240

ISBN: 978-0-02-145083-1
MHID: 0-02-145083-8

Printed in the United States of America.

10 11 12 13 KOD 24

Six pals met at ten.

All were best pals.

"A big van!" said Val.
All six pals spotted it.

Men were on the van's ramp.
"Let's visit that van," said Vick.

A kid was at the van.

The pals had never met him.

"I am Kevin," he said.

All six pals talked.
Kevin talked.

At ten, there were six best pals.
At eleven, there were seven!